Depression Era Kitchen Shakers

Schiffer® Publishing Ltd

4880 Lower Valley Road, Atglen, PA 19310 USA

Barbara E. Mauzy

12834354

Designed by Bonnie M. Hensley
Cover Designed by Bruce M. Waters
Type set in BernhardMod BT/Korinna BT

ISBN: 0-7643-1226-X
Printed in China
1 2 3 4

Published by Schiffer Publishing Ltd.
4880 Lower Valley Road
Atglen, PA 19310
Phone: (610) 593-1777; Fax: (610) 593-2002
E-mail: Schifferbk@aol.com
Please visit our web site catalog at **www.schifferbooks.com**

In Europe, Schiffer books are distributed by Bushwood Books
6 Marksbury Avenue Kew Gardens
Surrey TW9 4JF England
Phone: 44 (0) 20-8392-8585; Fax: 44 (0) 20-8392-9876
E-mail: Bushwd@aol.com
Free postage in the UK. Europe: air mail at cost.

This book may be purchased from the publisher.
Include $3.95 for shipping. Please try your bookstore first.
We are always looking for people to write books on new and related subjects.
If you have an idea for a book please contact us at the above address.
You may write for a free catalog.

Contents

Dutch

Flowers

Fruit Basket

Garden Gate with Tree

Hats

Lady Churning Butter

Lady Watering Flowers

Leaves

Acknowledgement & Dedication

Somewhere north of the bustle of the Big Apple, south of the New England Pines, east of the calming sound, and west of the rolling waves one can find the impressive collection of Patricia M. Zeman. "Patty Z." has devoted herself to creating and displaying a wonderful assortment of milk glass spice shakers, which I am delighted to present in this book. We met almost ten years ago in my shop over a set of shakers and we've gone from a seller-buyer relationship to that of close friends. Her career in drafting and engineering spilled into her collection: for years dealers and collectors have been privileged to see her famous catalogue of shakers; the truly honored were given their own copies. Without her expertise, input, guidance, and of course glassware, this book would not exist. My deepest thanks to a dear friend! This acknowledgement is a surprise so the acknowledged will be surprised and the surprised become the acknowledged, so Patty: this one's for you!

How to Use This Book

This book is designed as a guide to assist in building and managing a shaker collection. Check-off boxes are provided to allow one to keep careful and accurate track of the shakers owned and/or needed. If you find shakers I have not included, I encourage you to write directly in your book. Likewise, please contact me so if there is ever a need for an updated book it will be as complete as possible.

About the Shakers

All of the shakers presented in this book have lithographs applied to glass. There are no decals in this collection. Shakers with grooves at the corners are usually made by Tipp City and will be so marked on the bottoms. Tipp City shakers will usually also say "Made in U.S.A." McKee Glass Company makes Roman Arch shakers. Shakers with "DOVE" paper labels on the back were distributed by The Frank Tea and Spice Company and normally have a concave ring on the bottom. The prices shown in this book do not account for any additional value for paper labels.

About the Prices

This book is designed to be a tool, and hopefully both a fun and helpful one. Values vary immensely according to the condition of the piece, the location of the market, and the overall quality of the design and manufacture. Condition and availability is of paramount importance in assigning a value. The prices listed in this book are for individual items that are in mint condition, but not necessarily with original lids. Prices in the Midwest differ from those in the West or East, and those at specialty shows will vary from those at general shows. And, of course, being at the right place at the right time can make all the difference. The effect of online auctions cannot be ignored. Prices of these shakers have risen sharply in the past two years largely due to this global marketplace. Everything possible has been done to provide realistic prices, but it is impossible to create an absolutely accurate price list. I offer a guide that reflects what one could expect to pay.

If a shaker still has the original paper label in excellent condition the value should be increased $5-10. Shakers having a design on multiple sides are also worth $5-10 more than the same shakers with a design only on the front.

Neither the author nor the publisher is responsible for any outcomes resulting from consulting this book.

The Question of Lids

Old versus New, Original Paint versus Repainted

The question of lids and condition is truly a personal one and secondary to the condition of the glass and design on the glass. Some collectors insist on original lids, others will buy a shaker that is needed to complete a set even if it has no lid. There is no right or wrong, it is truly a matter of personal taste. However, if one waits for original lids in excellent condition it will be quite difficult to create a collection. These shakers were used, and I suspect few grandmothers ever considered protecting them for posterity.

Many of the lids shown in this book have been repainted, and many are replacement lids as this collector was interested in the aesthetics of her collection.

The Question of Size

How to Measure Your Shakers

Every effort was made to provide accurate, usable measurements. The numbers provided do not include the shaker lids. Dimensions were taken from the base of each shaker to the top of the rim. Wherever possible these figures are written to the quarter inch. There were a few shakers that had to be measured to the eighth inch.

How to Reach the Author

I certainly reply most promptly to e-mails. Please note that I will not open any e-mail with an attachment. If you wish to share an image, print it and sent it via Snail Mail. For a written response please enclose either your e-mail address or a self-addressed stamped envelope. Thanks!

E-mail: TPTT@aol.com
Website: www.TPTT.net
eBay seller ID: TPTT@aol.com

Barbara E. Mauzy
PO Box 207
Akron, PA 17501

The Shakers

Apples (3")

☐ Salt $20-25
☐ Pepper $20-25

Batchelor Brothers (4.5")

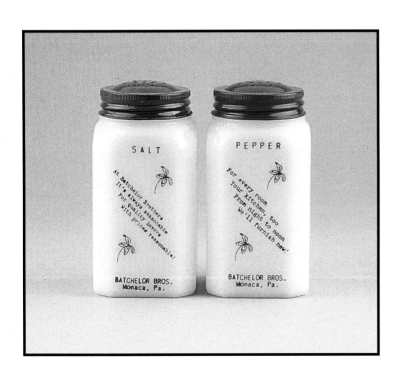

☐ Salt $50-60
☐ Pepper $50-60

   Note: Batchelor Brothers was a men's clothing store near Pittsburgh, PA.

Birds

Black Birds with Green Wings, Green Circle and Green Name (3")

- ☐ Salt $35-40
- ☐ Pepper $35-40

Note: These shakers have decorations on all four sides.

Black Birds with Red Wings, Red Circle and Red Name (3")

- ☐ Salt $45-50
- ☐ Pepper $45-50
- ☐ Flour (not shown) $60-65
- ☐ Sugar (not shown) $60-65

Note: The red set is more rare than the green set, and these only have decorations on the front.

Black Birds, Black Name at Bottom (4.5")

- ☐ Salt $50-60
- ☐ Pepper $50-60
- ☐ Sugar (not shown) $60-65
- ☐ Butter dish/grease jar $125-150

Note: This is an extremely rare set.

Blue Swans, Red Name at Bottom (3")

☐ Salt $10-15
☐ Pepper $10-15

Orange & Green Roosters, Black Name at Top

2.75" Size

- ☐ Salt $20-25
- ☐ Pepper $20-25
- ☐ Flour $20-25
- ☐ Sugar $20-25
- ☐ Allspice $20-25
- ☐ Cinnamon $20-25
- ☐ Cloves $20-25
- ☐ Ginger $20-25
- ☐ Mustard $20-25
- ☐ Nutmeg $20-25
- ☐ Paprika $20-25
- ☐ Red Pepper $20-25

4" size

- ☐ Salt $25-30
- ☐ Pepper $25-30
- ☐ Flour $25-30
- ☐ Sugar $25-30

Butterflies (4")

- ☐ Salt $45-50
- ☐ Pepper $45-50
- ☐ Flour $45-50
- ☐ Sugar (not shown) $45-50

Cattails

2.75" Size
- ☐ Salt $15-20
- ☐ Pepper $15-20
- ☐ Flour (not shown) $15-20
- ☐ Sugar (not shown) $15-20

Note: Add $5-10 per shaker for decorations on all four sides.

4" Size

- ☐ Salt $20-25
- ☐ Pepper $20-25
- ☐ Flour $20-25
- ☐ Sugar $20-25

Note: The 2.75" size is also available with green cattails and green writing found straight across at the top, not on an angle as shown in these.

Cherries

Red Cherries with Green Leaves, Red Name at Top

2.75" Size
- ☐ Salt $15-20
- ☐ Pepper $15-20
- ☐ Flour $15-20
- ☐ Sugar $15-20

☐ Butter dish/grease jar $125-150

Note: Add $5-10 per shaker for decorations on all four sides.

- ☐ Allspice $15-20
- ☐ Cinnamon $15-20
- ☐ Cloves $15-20
- ☐ Ginger $15-20
- ☐ Mustard $15-20
- ☐ Nutmeg $15-20
- ☐ Paprika $15-20
- ☐ Red Pepper $15-20

4"Size

- ☐ Pepper $30-35
- ☐ Sugar $30-35
- ☐ Flour $30-35
- ☐ Cinnamon $30-35

Red Cherries with Black Leaves, Red Name at Top

3" Size
- ☐ Cinnamon $25-30
- ☐ Flour $25-30
- ☐ Pepper $25-30
- ☐ Sugar $25-30

4" Size
- ☐ Salt (not shown) $30-35
- ☐ Pepper (not shown) $30-35
- ☐ Flour (not shown) $30-35
- ☐ Sugar (not shown) $30-35

Dogs

Black Scottie, Black Name at Top (2.75")

- ☐ Salt $45-50
- ☐ Pepper $45-50
- ☐ Flour $45-50
- ☐ Sugar (not shown) $45-50

- ☐ Allspice $50-60
- ☐ Celery $50-60
- ☐ Cinnamon $50-60
- ☐ Cloves $50-60
- ☐ Dill $50-60
- ☐ Ginger $50-60
- ☐ Mustard $50-60
- ☐ Nutmeg $50-60
- ☐ Onion $50-60
- ☐ Paprika $50-60
- ☐ Red Pepper $50-60
- ☐ Sage $50-60
- ☐ Butter dish/grease jar $150-175

Note: This is the most common of the three Scottie styles.

Black Scottie, Red Name at Top (3")

- ☐ Salt $50-60
- ☐ Pepper $50-60
- ☐ Flour $50-60
- ☐ Sugar (not shown) $50-60

Three Black Scotties, Black Name at Top on an Angle (4")

- ☐ Salt $65-75
- ☐ Pepper $65-75
- ☐ Flour $65-75
- ☐ Sugar $65-75

Three Black Scotties, Black Name at Top on a curve (4.5")

- ☐ Salt $65-75
- ☐ Pepper $65-75
- ☐ Flour (not shown) $65-75
- ☐ Sugar (not shown) $65-75

White Westie (my Moxie), Black Name at Top

3"Size

- ☐ Salt $45-50
- ☐ Pepper $45-50
- ☐ Flour $45-50
- ☐ Sugar $45-50

- ☐ Cinnamon $50-60
- ☐ Paprika $50-60

Note: Add $5-10 per shaker for decorations on all four sides.

4.5" Size

- ☐ Salt (not shown) $65-75
- ☐ Pepper (not shown) $65-75
- ☐ Flour (not shown) $65-75
- ☐ Sugar (not shown) $65-75

Note: The 4.5" size is quite rare.

Dutch

Blue Figures, Red Name at Bottom with "Fan" Sides (3")

☐ Salt $10-12
☐ Pepper $10-12
☐ Sugar $10-12

Note: This has been found in the original box and did not include a Flour shaker. These shakers have a "fan" design in the glass on the sides.

Blue Figures, Red Name at Bottom with Smooth Sides, (3")
Similar to Dutch design with red diamond

- ☐ Allspice (girl in boat) $15-20
- ☐ Allspice (girl & boy) $10-12
- ☐ Chili Powder (lady with kettle) $10-12
- ☐ Cinnamon (girl with pail) $10-12
- ☐ Cinnamon (girl with two pails) $10-12
- ☐ Cinnamon (girl with potted tulip-not shown) $15-20
- ☐ Cloves (girl with hoop) $15-20
- ☐ Cloves (boy with boat in two hands) $10-12
- ☐ Cloves (boy with boat in one hand) $10-12
- ☐ Ginger (girl with goose) $10-12

- ☐ Mace (lady with spinning wheel) $15-20
- ☐ Mustard (boy with fishing pole) $10-12
- ☐ Mustard (boy on scooter) $15-20
- ☐ Nutmeg (man and boy)$10-12
- ☐ Paprika (dancing lady) $10-12
- ☐ Red Pepper ("Mexican" head) $10-12
- ☐ White Pepper (ice skating boy) $15-20

Note: This is a complex design as variations of the same spice are available. These are always printed in blue and have red names at the bottom.

Blue Figures, Blue Name at Top (3")

Medium Blue
- ☐ Salt $10-15
- ☐ Pepper $10-15

Darker Blue
- ☐ Salt $20-25
- ☐ Pepper $20-25

Note: The darker blue set is much more rare than the medium blue set. The figures and letters on the dark blue are larger than those on the medium blue.

Blue Salt & Red Pepper, Blue & Red Name at Bottom

3" Size
- ☐ Salt $20-25
- ☐ Pepper $20-25

4.5" Size
- ☐ Salt $20-25
- ☐ Pepper $20-25

Dancing Couple, Black or Blue Name at Bottom (3")

Red & Black Figures, Black Name at Bottom
- ☐ Salt $20-25
- ☐ Pepper $20-25
- ☐ Flour $20-25

- ☐ Sugar $20-25

- ☐ Cinnamon $25-30
- ☐ Paprika $25-30

Blue & Orange Figures, Blue Name at Bottom

- ☐ Salt $30-35
- ☐ Pepper $30-35
- ☐ Flour (not shown) $30-35
- ☐ Sugar (not shown) $30-35

Four Color Set (Slim), Blue, Red, Orange, & Green Name at Bottom (3 5/8")

Smaller Letters

- ☐ Salt (blue) $25-30
- ☐ Pepper (red) $25-30
- ☐ Flour (orange) $35-40
- ☐ Sugar (green) $35-40

Larger Letters
- ☐ Salt (blue) $20-25
- ☐ Pepper (red) $20-25

Lady with Carrots, Name at Top (3")

- ☐ Salt (blue) $15-20
- ☐ Pepper (red) $15-20

No Diamond, Name at Top (3")

- ☐ Cream of Tartar $20-25
- ☐ Curry Powder $20-25
- ☐ Seasoning Salt $20-25

Note: These shakers are rare.

Red Diamond on Top, Name at Top (3")

- ☐ Salt $10-12
- ☐ Pepper $10-12

- ☐ Allspice $10-12
- ☐ Celery Salt $15-20
- ☐ Chili Powder $15-20
- ☐ Cinnamon $10-12
- ☐ Cloves $10-12
- ☐ Garlic Salt $10-12
- ☐ Ginger $10-12
- ☐ Mace $15-20
- ☐ Mustard $10-12
- ☐ Nutmeg $10-12
- ☐ Onion Salt $15-20
- ☐ Paprika $10-12

48

Red Pennsylvania Dutch Design, Red Name at Top (4.5")

- ☐ Roastmeat Seasoning $40-45
- ☐ Salt $30-35
- ☐ Pepper $30-35

Note: The lettering of the salt and pepper is also found tilted (italics) as shown on the Roastmeat Seasoning.

Running Figures, Name at Bottom (4.5")

- ☐ Salt (red) $30-35
- ☐ Pepper (red) $30-35
- ☐ Sugar (red- not shown) $40-45

Note: Sugar is only found in red.

- ☐ Salt (blue) $30-35
- ☐ Pepper (blue) $30-35

- ☐ Salt (green-not shown) $50-60
- ☐ Pepper (green-not shown) $50-60

Note: Green is an extremely rare set.

Windmills, Red Name at Bottom

3" Size
- ☐ Salt $10-15
- ☐ Pepper $10-15

4.5" Size
- ☐ Salt $15-20
- ☐ Pepper $15-20

Flowers

Daisies in Red "Swirled" Vase, Black Name at Top (4.5")

- ☐ Salt $20-25
- ☐ Pepper (not shown) $20-25
- ☐ Flour $20-25
- ☐ Sugar (not shown) $20-25

Orange Morning Glories, Green Name at Side (4.5")

- ☐ Salt $45-50
- ☐ Pepper $45-50
- ☐ Flour $45-50
- ☐ Sugar $45-50

Orange Flowers with "Mesh" Background, Black Name at Bottom (4.5")

- ☐ Salt $45-50
- ☐ Pepper $45-50
- ☐ Flour (not shown) $45-50
- ☐ Sugar (not shown) $45-50

Poinsettias, Black Name at Top

2.75"Size

- ☐ Salt (not shown) $25-30
- ☐ Pepper $25-30
- ☐ Flour $25-30
- ☐ Sugar $25-30

- ☐ Allspice $25-30
- ☐ Cinnamon $25-30
- ☐ Cloves $25-30
- ☐ Ginger $25-30
- ☐ Mustard $25-30
- ☐ Nutmeg $25-30
- ☐ Paprika $25-30
- ☐ Red Pepper $25-30
- ☐ Butter dish/grease jar $125-150

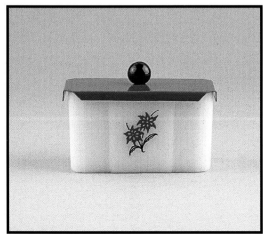

4" Size
- ☐ Salt $35-40
- ☐ Pepper $35-40
- ☐ Flour $35-40
- ☐ Sugar $35-40

Poinsettias, Black Name at Side (4")

- ☐ Salt $25-30
- ☐ Pepper $25-30
- ☐ Flour $25-30
- ☐ Sugar $25-30

Note: Smaller (2.75") size is also available but not pictured.

- ☐ Salt (not shown) $25-30
- ☐ Pepper (not shown) $25-30
- ☐ Flour (not shown) $25-30
- ☐ Sugar (not shown) $25-30

Red Blossoms in Black Basket, Black Name at Top

2.75"Size

- ☐ Salt $10-15
- ☐ Pepper $10-15
- ☐ Flour $10-15
- ☐ Sugar $10-15

- ☐ Allspice $10-15
- ☐ Celery $15-20
- ☐ Cinnamon $10-15
- ☐ Cloves $10-15
- ☐ Dill $15-20
- ☐ Garlic $15-20
- ☐ Ginger $10-15
- ☐ Mace $15-20
- ☐ Mustard $10-15
- ☐ Nutmeg $10-15
- ☐ Onion (not shown) $15-20
- ☐ Paprika $10-15
- ☐ Red Pepper $10-15
- ☐ Sage $15-20
- ☐ Butter dish/grease jar $125-150

60

4" Size

- ☐ Salt $25-30
- ☐ Pepper $25-30
- ☐ Flour $25-30
- ☐ Sugar $25-30

Note: Add $5-10 per shaker for decorations on all four sides.

Red Morning Glories, Red Name at Top

2.75" Size

- ☐ Cinnamon $20-25
- ☐ Cloves $20-25
- ☐ Flour (not shown) $20-25
- ☐ Mustard $20-25
- ☐ Paprika $20-25
- ☐ Pepper (not shown) $20-25
- ☐ Red Pepper $20-25
- ☐ Salt $20-25

4"Size

- ☐ Salt (not shown) $30-35
- ☐ Pepper (not shown) $30-35
- ☐ Flour $30-35
- ☐ Sugar $30-35

Red Blossoms with Large Black Leaves, Black Name at Top

2.5"Size

- ☐ Salt $15-20
- ☐ Pepper $15-20
- ☐ Flour $15-20
- ☐ Sugar $15-20

- ☐ Allspice $15-20
- ☐ Cinnamon $15-20
- ☐ Cloves $15-20
- ☐ Ginger $15-20
- ☐ Mustard $15-20
- ☐ Nutmeg $15-20
- ☐ Paprika $15-20
- ☐ Red Pepper $15-20
- ☐ Butter dish/grease jar $150-175

4" Size
- ☐ Salt $30-35
- ☐ Pepper $30-35
- ☐ Flour $30-35
- ☐ Sugar $30-35

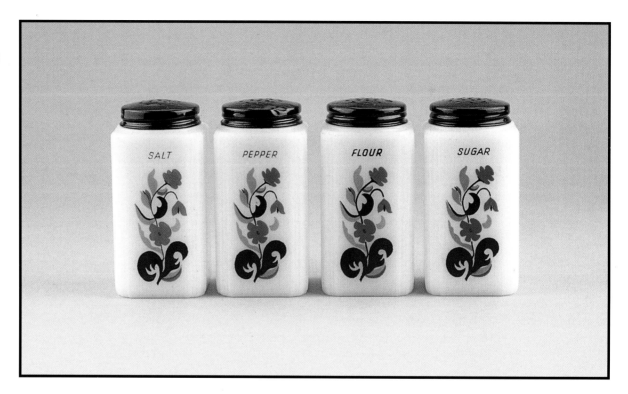

Red Blossoms with Green Leaves, Black Name at Top

2.75" Size
- ☐ Salt (not shown) $20-25
- ☐ Pepper $20-25
- ☐ Flour $20-25
- ☐ Sugar $20-25

- ☐ Cinnamon $20-25

4" Size
- ☐ Salt $30-35
- ☐ Pepper $30-35
- ☐ Flour (not shown) $30-35
- ☐ Sugar (not shown) $30-35

Small Orange Blossoms, Vertical Green Name at Side (3")

☐ Salt $30-35
☐ Pepper $30-35

Note: These have a design on all four sides.

Small Red Blossoms, Vertical Black Name at Side

2.75"Size (grooves at corners)
- ☐ Salt $10-15
- ☐ Pepper $10-15
- ☐ Flour $10-15
- ☐ Sugar $10-15

- ☐ Cinnamon $10-15
- ☐ Paprika $10-15

3" Size (no grooves at corners)
- ☐ Salt $10-15
- ☐ Pepper $10-15
- ☐ Flour $10-15
- ☐ Sugar (not shown) $10-15

- ☐ Cinnamon $10-15

Note: Add $5-10 per shaker for decorations on all four sides.

4" Size
- ☐ Salt $15-20
- ☐ Pepper $15-20
- ☐ Flour $15-20
- ☐ Sugar $15-20

4.5" Size
- ☐ Salt $15-20
- ☐ Pepper $15-20
- ☐ Flour $15-20
- ☐ Sugar $15-20

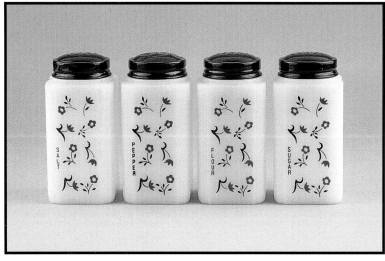

Tiny Red Flowers with Twisting Vines, Black Name at Side

2.75"Size
- ☐ Salt $10-15
- ☐ Pepper $10-15
- ☐ Flour $10-15
- ☐ Sugar (not shown) $10-15

4" Size
- ☐ Salt (not shown) $15-20
- ☐ Pepper (not shown) $15-20
- ☐ Flour $15-20
- ☐ Sugar $15-20

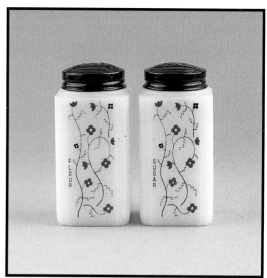

Tulips, Red Name in Middle (3")

- ☐ Salt $15-20
- ☐ Pepper $15-20
- ☐ Flour $15-20
- ☐ Sugar $15-20

- ☐ Cinnamon $15-20
- ☐ Paprika $15-20

Tulips, Green Name Near Bottom (3")

- ☐ Salt $10-15
- ☐ Pepper $10-15

Two Flowers in a Red Pot, Black Name in Middle (4.5")

- ☐ Pepper $50-60
- ☐ Salt $50-60
- ☐ Sugar (not shown) $50-60
- ☐ Butter dish/grease jar $150-175

Yellow Daisy with Red Geranium, Green Name at Top

2.75"Size

- ☐ Salt $30-35
- ☐ Pepper $30-35
- ☐ Flour $30-35
- ☐ Sugar $30-35

- ☐ Allspice $30-35
- ☐ Cinnamon $30-35
- ☐ Cloves $30-35
- ☐ Ginger $30-35
- ☐ Mustard $30-35
- ☐ Nutmeg $30-35
- ☐ Paprika $30-35
- ☐ Red Pepper $30-35

4" Size
- ☐ Salt $30-35
- ☐ Pepper $30-35
- ☐ Flour $30-35
- ☐ Sugar $30-35

Yellow Flowers with Red Flowers, Red Name at Top

2.75"Size
- ☐ Salt $30-35
- ☐ Pepper $30-35
- ☐ Flour $30-35
- ☐ Sugar (not shown) $30-35

- ☐ Allspice $30-35
- ☐ Cinnamon $30-35
- ☐ Cloves $30-35
- ☐ Ginger $30-35
- ☐ Mustard $30-35
- ☐ Nutmeg $30-35
- ☐ Paprika $30-35
- ☐ Red Pepper $30-35

4" Size

- ☐ Salt $30-35
- ☐ Pepper $30-35
- ☐ Flour $30-35
- ☐ Sugar $30-35

Note: The letters on the 4" size are black, not red as on the smaller size.

Fruit Basket

Fruit in Basket, Black Name at Top

2.75" Size
- ☐ Salt $30-35
- ☐ Pepper $30-35
- ☐ Butter dish/grease jar $175-200 (not shown)

4" Size
- ☐ Salt (not shown) $45-50
- ☐ Pepper (not shown) $45-50

Garden Gate with Tree

Gate & Tree, Black Name at Bottom

3" Size
- ☐ Salt $25-30
- ☐ Pepper $25-30
- ☐ Flour $25-30
- ☐ Sugar (not shown) $25-30
- ☐ Butter dish/grease jar $125-150

Note: Add $5-10 per shaker for decorations on all four sides.

4.5" Size

- ☐ Salt $35-40
- ☐ Pepper $35-40
- ☐ Flour $35-40
- ☐ Sugar $35-40

Hats

Uncle Sam Hats, Name Near Top (3")

- ☐ Salt $20-25
- ☐ Pepper $20-25

Note: This version has a completely blue salt and a completely red pepper which is much more rare than the other Uncle Sam Hats.

Blue & Red Uncle Sam Hats, Red Name Near Top (3")

- ☐ Salt $10-15
- ☐ Pepper $10-15

Note: This version has blue hats at the bottom of both the salt and the pepper.

Lady Churning Butter

Blue Salt & Red Pepper, Blue & Red Name at Bottom (slim, 3-5/8")

- ☐ Salt (blue) $25-30
- ☐ Pepper (red) $25-30

Blue Salt & Red Pepper, Blue & Red Name at Bottom with Garland Ring (4.5")

- ☐ Salt (blue) $20-25
- ☐ Pepper (red) $20-25

Lady Watering Flowers

Black Outline of Lady, Black Name at Top on Angle

2.75" Size
- ☐ Salt $20-25
- ☐ Pepper $20-25
- ☐ Flour $20-25
- ☐ Sugar $20-25

- ☐ Cinnamon $20-25
- ☐ Cloves $20-25
- ☐ Ginger $20-25
- ☐ Mustard $20-25
- ☐ Nutmeg $20-25
- ☐ Paprika $20-25
- ☐ Red Pepper $20-25

☐ Butter dish/grease jar $150-175

Note: Salt and Pepper are the only shakers with red embellishments. Add $5-10 per shaker for decorations on all four sides.

84

4" Size

- ☐ Salt $20-25
- ☐ Pepper $20-25
- ☐ Flour $20-25
- ☐ Sugar $20-25

Note: Add $5-10 per shaker for decorations on all four sides.

Black Outline of Lady, Black Name at Top with Slight Curve (3")

- ☐ Salt (not shown) $20-25
- ☐ Pepper (not shown) $20-25
- ☐ Flour $20-25
- ☐ Sugar $20-25

Note: All four of these shakers have red embellishments.

Black Outline of Lady, Black Name at Top on Curve

4.5" Size
- ☐ Salt $35-40
- ☐ Pepper $35-40
- ☐ Flour $35-40
- ☐ Sugar (not shown) $35-40

- ☐ Allspice (not shown) $35-40
- ☐ Cinnamon (not shown) $35-40
- ☐ Cloves $35-40
- ☐ Ginger (not shown) $35-40
- ☐ Nutmeg (not shown) $35-40
- ☐ Paprika (not shown) $35-40

Note: All shakers in this size have red embellishments.

Leaves

Black Maple Leaves, Black Letters Near Top

3" Size
- ☐ Salt $40-45
- ☐ Pepper $40-45

4.5" Size
- ☐ Salt (not shown) $50-60
- ☐ Pepper (not shown) $50-60

Note: Add $5-10 per shakers for decorations on all four sides.

Red Maple Leaves, Red Name at Bottom (4.5")

- ☐ Salt $40-45
- ☐ Pepper $40-45

Mexican

Red Figure, Red Name at Side (4.5")

- ☐ Salt $50-60
- ☐ Pepper $50-60
- ☐ Butter dish/grease jar $175-200 (not shown)

Note: These pieces are extremely rare.

Red Figure, Red Name at Top (3")

- ☐ Allspice $30-35
- ☐ Cinnamon $30-35
- ☐ Garlic Salt $30-35
- ☐ Nutmeg $30-35

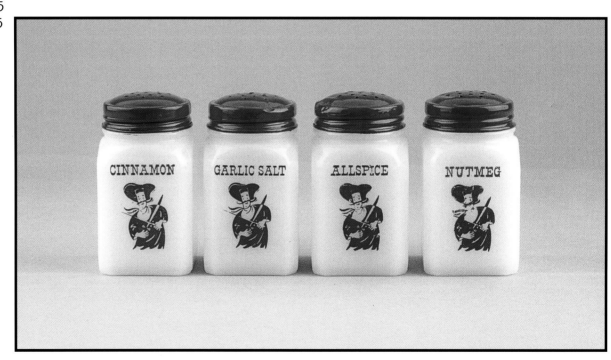

Niagara Falls

Blue Salt & Red Pepper, Blue & Red Names at Bottom (3")

- ☐ Salt (blue image with red name) $10-12
- ☐ Pepper (red image with blue name) $10-12

Rings

Blue Rings, Blue Name in Middle (3-3/8")

- ☐ Salt $10-15
- ☐ Pepper $10-15

Sailboats

Blue & Red Ships, Blue & Red Name at Bottom (3")

- ☐ Salt (blue with red letters) $10-15
- ☐ Pepper (red with blue letters) $10-15

Red Ships, Red Name at Bottom (3")

- ☐ Salt $10-15
- ☐ Pepper $10-15

Green Ships, Green Name at Bottom (3")

- ☐ Salt $15-20
- ☐ Pepper $15-20

Note: Of all the Sailboat designs this is the most rare.

Red Ships, Red Name at Top
(McKee Roman Arch, 3-5/8")

- ☐ Salt $25-30
- ☐ Pepper $25-30
- ☐ Flour $25-30
- ☐ Sugar $25-30

Note: Of all the Sailboat designs this is in the most demand. There are two correct lids for this set: metal and plastic.

The Herb Chest (3")

Blue Design, Blue Name at Top

- ☐ Bay Leaves $20-25
- ☐ Marjoram $20-25
- ☐ Oregano $20-25
- ☐ Parsley $20-25
- ☐ Poultry Seasoning $20-25

- ☐ Rosemary $20-25
- ☐ Sage $20-25
- ☐ Savory $20-25
- ☐ Thyme $20-25

Note: These are quite rare.

The Spice Chest (3")

Blue Dutch Motif, Blue Name at top

- ☐ Salt $15-20
- ☐ Pepper $15-20

- ☐ Allspice $15-20
- ☐ Cinnamon $15-20
- ☐ Cloves $15-20
- ☐ Ginger $15-20
- ☐ Mustard $15-20
- ☐ Nutmeg $15-20

Note: These shakers have a "fan" design in the glass on the sides.